Celebrate Spring
Planting Seeds

by Kathryn Clay

CAPSTONE PRESS
a capstone imprint

Little Pebble is published by Capstone Press,
1710 Roe Crest Drive, North Mankato, Minnesota 56003
www.mycapstone.com

Library of Congress Cataloging-in-Publication Data
Clay, Kathryn, author.
  Planting seeds / by Kathryn Clay.
    pages cm.—(Little pebble. Celebrate spring)
  Summary: "Simple nonfiction text and full-color photographs present planting seeds in spring"—Provided by the publisher.
  Audience: Ages 5–7.
  Audience: K to grade 3.
  Includes bibliographical references and index.
  ISBN 978-1-4914-8305-3 (library binding)
  ISBN 978-1-4914-8309-1 (paperback)
  ISBN 978-1-4914-8313-8 (ebook pdf)
1. Seeds—Juvenile literature. 2. Gardening—Juvenile literature. 3. Spring—Juvenile literature.
I. Title.
  QK661.C53 2016
  635—dc23   2015023305

Editorial Credits
Erika L. Shores, editor; Juliette Peters and Ashlee Suker, designers;
Svetlana Zhurkin, media researcher; Katy LaVigne, production specialist

Photo Credits
Capstone Studio: Karon Dubke, cover; Dreamstime: Branex, 15, Wally Stemberger, 7; Getty Images: Superstudio, 21; iStockphoto: MKucova, 1; Newscom: Blend Images/KidStock, 19; Shutterstock: Africa Studio, 3, caldix, 13, Filipe B. Varela, 9, Maks Narodenko, 15 (inset), Pressmaster, 17, Stockr, 5, TwilightArtPictures, 11, USBFCO, back cover and throughout

Table of Contents

Spring Is Here!

Cold winter weather ends.

It's time to plant seeds.

From Seed to Plant

Seeds need rain and sun.

Spring storms water the seeds.

Seeds crack open.

Roots push down.

Seeds push up from the soil.

They are called shoots.

Green leaves grow.

Small buds form.

Then the flowers bloom.

Who Plants Seeds?

A farmer plants seeds.

Corn grows tall in fields.

A gardener plants seeds.

She grows food in her backyard.

Ms. Rosa's class plants seeds.

They grow grass.

Luis and his dad plant seeds.
They grow flowers.

What seeds will you plant?

Glossary

bloom—to produce a flower

bud—the part of a plant that turns into a leaf or flower

root—the part of a plant that attaches to the ground

seed—a tiny plant part from which a new plant grows

shoot—the stem growing out of a seed that becomes the plant

Read More

Fogliano, Julie. *And Then It's Spring.* New York: Roaring Brook Press, 2012.

Rattini, Kristin Baird. *Seed to Plant.* National Geographic Readers. Washington, D.C.: National Geographic, 2014.

Rustad, Martha E. H. *Plants in Spring.* All About Spring. North Mankato, Minn.: Capstone Press, 2013.

Internet Sites

FactHound offers a safe, fun way to find Internet sites related to this book. All of the sites on FactHound have been researched by our staff.

Here's all you do:
Visit *www.facthound.com*
Type in this code: 9781491483053

Check out projects, games and lots more at
www.capstonekids.com

Index